Your journe
can end he

I cheat none but a worse death
in some ratslicked dungeon
or dropped in the pesthole,
death's shilling in my armpit.
● HAWKWOOD

contents

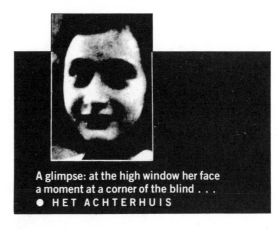

A glimpse: at the high window her face
a moment at a corner of the blind . . .
● HET ACHTERHUIS

You get loose teeth talking like that.
You're taking the fall, precious.
● BOGART IN THE DUMB WAITER

'So who cuts your hair, John?'

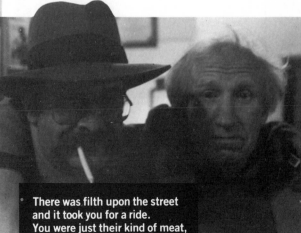

There was filth upon the street
and it took you for a ride.
You were just their kind of meat,
they were never on your side.

Only this time it never ends: the master
continually remarking how the weather bites cold,
the brandy flask stands empty, and the poor
are pushing to the windows like the fog.
● AFTER MR MAYHEW'S VISIT

THE LONDON POEMS

But all night I have been underwater
mining the harbours off Nicaragua,
I need a place to dress up in my uniform.
I have a deal for you. I'm your imaginary friend.
● YOUR FRIEND THE DRIFTER

HERE
LIES
Lester Moore
Four slugs
from A-44
No Les
No More

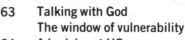

I'm primed, armed, fused, and now I'll tick
till I go off. Think of me as a deterrent.
● UNFINISHED PORTRAIT

I've joined the Rupert Bear School of Poetry
and I'll not say anything controversial.
● THE BOTANIC GARDEN OATH

terra

Copyright © Ken Smith 1986
All rights reserved

ISBN 0 906427 94 0

First published 1986 by
Bloodaxe Books Ltd,
P.O. Box 1SN,
Newcastle upon Tyne NE99 1SN.

Bloodaxe Books Ltd acknowledges
the financial assistance of Northern Arts.

Printed in Great Britain by
Tyneside Free Press Workshop Ltd,
Newcastle upon Tyne.

PHOTOGRAPHERS
Moira Conway
(back cover & adverts)
Allan Titmuss (inside front cover)
Ivor Bowen (front cover, inset)
Claire McNamee (inside back cover &
pages 2 & 5)
Jeremy Blank (page 4)
Stephen Parr (pages 51 & 52)

ARTISTS
Irene Reddish (cover illustration)
Peter Rider (portraits)
Paolo Uccello (Hawkwood)
Giovanni di Grassi (rat)

TYPESETTING
True North, Newcastle upon Tyne

DESIGN
Bloodaxe Books

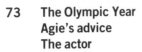

Acknowledgements

IGNORE PREVIOUS TELEGRAM

Poems from this book first appeared in the following publications: **Acumen**, **The Echo Room**, **Folio**, **Iron**, **Knjizevne Novine** (Belgrade), **Literary Review**, **London Magazine**, **London Review of Books**, **North** (Belfast), **Oxford Poetry**, **Pivot** (New York), **PN Review**, **Poetry Now/ Cambridge Poetry Magazine**, **Poetry Supplement** (Poetry Book Society, Christmas 1983), **Spectrum** and **Stand**. The section **IGNORE PREVIOUS PREVIOUS TELEGRAM** was published in the Arts for Labour anthology **Voices** (ed. Nicki Jackowska, Pluto Press, 1985).

HAWKWOOD, with incidental music commissioned from Michael Ball, was read by David Neal in a **BBC Radio 3** feature produced by Fraser Steel. 'After Mr Mayhew's visit', 'Not talking on the Circle Line', 'Beyond hope and the Lea River' and 'The Botanic Garden Oath' were broadcast in editions of **Poetry Now** (BBC Radio 3).

Six poems appeared in **The Quick Brown Fox**, a chapbook published by The Other Branch (Leamington Spa) in 1984, and fourteen of **THE LONDON POEMS** in **The House of Numbers** (Rolling Moss Press, 1985).

Once I was a puppy, a young poetrie apprentice
in the school of Whingeing Willy's blighted adolescence.
Now I get snotty letters from the likes of Anthony Thwaite,
my line is overextended. Is there no end to this?
● DEPARTURE'S SPEECH

H A W K W O O D

 IR JOHN HAWKWOOD, miles anglicus, 1320-1394: Born near Colchester in Essex, the younger son of a rich tanner who owned the manor of Sible Hedingham, Sir John Hawkwood died a citizen and freeman of Florence, where Uccello's equestrian fresco portrays him in the Duomo. He was, said Froissart, *a poor knight owning nothing but his spurs*, though he came to possess estates in the Romagna and Tuscany. A classic example of the younger son without inheritance who goes for a soldier, Hawkwood fought at Crécy and Poitiers, where he was knighted, early in the long English depred-

ations in France of what was not yet called the Hundred Years War.

Under the Black Prince, Hawkwood learned the tactics he was later to employ in Italy: mobility, forward intelligence and knowledge of the terrain, the devastating use of the longbow (a good bowman fired six

shafts a minute, the sixth in the air before the first found its target), and the dismounting of the lance, transforming the cavalry weapon of the mounted knight and squire into a two man infantry weapon, a third man holding the horses for swift pursuit or withdrawal.

In 1360 the Treaty of Bretigny suspended hostilities between England and France, the armies were paid off in the field, and the free

companies turned to plunder. Sixty thousand of these *routiers* went down the Rhône to Avignon *to visit the Pope and have some of his money.* They were known as *skinners.* Gascons, Bretons, Burgundians, Germans, Scots, Irish, Dutch, Flemings, Welsh, Cornish, French and English they were *those villains commonly called English, who wasted all the country without cause, and robbed without sparing all that ever they could get, and violated and defiled women, old and young, and slew men, women and children without mercy.* After their passing, it was said, *the forests came back.*

Hawkwood was amongst them, and appears in Italy in 1364 as the elected captain of the White Company, so called for the brightness of their armour, fighting for Pisa against Florence. Like most campaigns it was short, the Florentines bought off most of the Pisan mercenaries, including the bulk of Hawkwood's men, and the White

Company disintegrated. Hawkwood himself would not be bribed to ignore his contract. He was, by all accounts, very particular on this principle.

OVER THE NEXT 30 YEARS Hawkwood was a mercenary and fought variously as a condottiere, a contractor providing his own forces for one side or another amongst the Pisans, the Milanese, the Papal States, Padua, Naples, and Florence. For the latter half of this period he was on contract to Florence, while free to undertake other commissions.

Many of his victories were gained by stealth and deception; he was as adept at avoiding conflict as at entering it, as efficient in the timely withdrawal as in advance or ambush. His reputation in an age of cruel men was said to be brave, fair, merciful and honest in his dealings, and little of the wealth that came his way stayed with him. His reputation rested on his military skill and on his principle that a contract was a contract.

In 1376 while in the employ of the Papal States and under the orders of Robert of Geneva, Papal Legate in Rome and later Clement VII, first of the Anti-Popes, Hawkwood was

instructed to *administer justice* on the city of Cesena. Asked for clarification, the representative of Christ's representative on Earth replied he wanted *sangue et sangue: blood and more blood*. Whether in fulfilment of his contract ('obeying orders'), or whether as a means of paying his men in loot what his paymaster stood in arrears of, or whether had he refused his men would merely have elected a new commander, Hawkwood obeyed. The citizens having first been persuaded to surrender their arms, for three days the people of Cesena were systematically slaughtered, the town looted, and what could not be carried off destroyed.

IN OUR TERMS, Hawkwood was a war criminal, responsible for an atrocity. Shortly thereafter he left papal service and began his long association with Florence.

He was twice married, the second time to Donnina, one of the many offspring of Bernabo Visconti. For some years he lived the life of a country squire such as he might have lived in Essex, though at the age of 70 he was still campaigning.

In 1387, fighting for Padua against Verona, he scored a decisive victory at Castagnaro, and in 1389 he undertook a forced march from Naples when summoned back to Florence. When he died in 1394 he was buried not in the tomb prepared for him in Florence and subsequently memorialised by Uccello, but at the request of Richard II in Sible Hedingham, the village where he was born, in a grave that has now been lost. *KS*

HAWKWOOD

(for Eric Willcocks)

Do ye nat knowe that living by warre
peece wold be my undoeing?
● H A W K W O O D

There is ful many a man that crieth Werre! Werre!
that wot ful litel what werre amounteth.
● **CHAUCER**

Seated, a man with the tools of his trade,
solitary in the company of weapons,
always the warrior, apart,
etched into metal in a moment of brooding.

Mostly he sleeps sound till first light,
by day lives the life of his time:
fighting to live he will fight
for cash money or credit. Or not fight.

At his ease when he may be,
who can never go home now,
his landscape the blunt northerly speech
glimpsed through the window to his left

where the hills are already going to sleep,
the road hatched away into more shadow
always closing round him. In the foreground
a single candle he has lit against the night.

Messer Giovanni condottiere
I thinke this worlde a boke
and wolde rede it

turning back the pages
chapter by century
into the distant background

where all that's certain now
has already happened –
an argument for lawyers,

each day's skin
stitched to another day's drum,
another season of wheat,

another year of tramped corpses,
some words falling away
for instance *brother, victim.*

Who knows what any of it was now?
I move between the dead and the dead,
always erudite and fractious,

in their different speech the same:
the same dangerous commonwealth, men
totting up loot, stacked heads,

the harvest of scrap metal
at the engagement's end, some thrush
puncturing the heavy noon air.

Thereafter come the keening women,
gulls to pick out eyes,
the broken citizenry in halters.

A long tale the same again sir
repeating itself *o misere misere*,
burning what we could not steal.

In truth sirs
I merely disable myself
in this condotta with words,

so many flags
under conflicting allegiance,
meanings that dodge

across factions and borders,
lights over the marshland,
smoke or the shiftings of water.

Men's speech is all cunning,
bragging and grief.
We must make some agreement.

And honour it,
clause by condition,
down to the letter.

At the eye of all shadow
if I sleep by the tallow's grace
I sleep wretchedly. My heart
flies out of my mouth and away.

She is perched singing all alone
in the plane trees by the river,
all thought of this quick planet
sweet even in war snuffed out.

One wall of fire sweeps the vineyards.
All men are with women instantly angels
vapoured in swift rising air,
their bodies shriven in sharp metal.

This is my skull's dream. Meanwhile
my heart stretches wings over woods
singing out of our childhood once
in the abrupt speech of my own land.

And this I do is my dreamwork
late and unwilling, the watch
posted alert, rattle of irons,
long deathcry of some creature

caught in the hedgeback alone, stars
and the moon's pale face over all.
My heart goes away, flying north
to the snowy passes she will die in.

Night by night she is fainter,
further and colder, her voice
in the star maze at the far range
of my hearing.
                    Where I

working late and close to the page
draw up the sketch for a medallion:
my heart between a falcon's claws,
my name *Acuto* and the versant writ

What am I but a vicious labourer,
the iron grub that kills for pay?
What I am now so you will be.
What you are now so I was once.

Awake and sweating in my flesh,
my heart gone off without my leave
perhaps for better pay elsewhere.

Or she must beg her way
through warring neighbourhoods alone,
and like me sell her only skin.

Or limp a penitent to Rome
whose bishop is one of two great lechers
and I but one of his butchers.

Between the birthstool and the planks.
Between the slippery dialects:
Auti, Auguto, Giovanni Awkward

*sharpen your good blade, shine
in your beaten armour, get horse
and a good ship ready and go home.*

I am a blank slate on which is set
menace and *oblivion*. I sit
witness to the witch's wick
studied in the candle's hiss.

I make war because there is no work in England
and profit from necessity.
I who have privatised war,
I have made of my life great industry.

These cities made of fluencies
and money, rich hinterlands
stood into wheat, the ripe grapes
bell and split their juices:

all mine now. I who reap stones
from a seedcorn of ashes,
I who grind out the future
between millstone and millstone address you.

You who live between knife and cut
and hone the blade, dragging wood
across a muddy evening home,
another day with nowt to show.

You will come to the harvest of swords
the same. You who nurse the heart
in its ladle of blood and sing
lullabies to the love you lost, you also

to the pit's rim, tar hissing and the devils
delighting in your misery, all fire
suddenly upon you, the preliminary routine
of rape and mutilation done, they will kill you.

Your moment in the sunlight will be over,
the sparrow fleeting at the yard end,
some field you walked beside the river
between the willows and the ripened wheat.

I mark the changes: *none* and *none*.
Some day between some years of peace
we hear fighting break out in the valley
and the unending warfare comes home.

A river known by many names: *The War*
or *The Rocking Horse Expedition*
or *The Campaign of the Seven Brown Loaves*,
it is the same miserable waterway

we dream the river that will drown us.
They say dreaming is to forget,
in which case I have forgot much.
My dreams show clear them I killed –

in a three day butchery at Cesena
a nun I halved from neck to waist
from worse between squabbling soldiers.
I, Giovanni Haukkuode, did this.

Who might have been anyone,
a tanner yellow with the lifelong stink
of burning dog muck, a pilgrim
limping to Jerusalem and back.

I might have lived my days
in some slope of the hills,
a man reckoning fleece,
hides for the Lowlands, wineskins.

I am a man becoming an emblem,
inscribing the book of his name
who must shift across ploughlands
because no one will have him at home.

I chart the cries of other sleepers:
one a fat drunk cherub must have *sangue sangue*,
another has designed an engine
to flatten cities and will use it.

Another weeps he is the King of France
and mad and made of clear glass
and will break. His cry
a wounded man's, a pierced bird's.

Some nights the blood rush at my temple
hammers *you will die you will die.*
I see white images of the ditch
at Castagnaro heaving maggots.

Pink and fleshly, they are cribs
of black flies everywhere in Europe,
the arrow shower, the lance thicket,
nails of the cross everyone walks with.

My enemy sends a caged fox for taunt.
I let him go. I take hawk and horse
and ride to inspect the fortifications.
Later I will rally all with my cry

Carne Carne, given to the meatwork.
And where's my heart? Friend,
I dream she is in a far country,
her message fading as it finds me.

Persistent as the rust in unused iron,
from The Serene Republic of Slaughtered Innocents
and The Most Royal Kingdom of Branded Thieves
my heart sends greetings.

My heart sends coin to pay for all,
meat and the red sleepy wine of Genoa,
bed and a fresh horse at sunrise:
Signor sithee take cash

in fair dealing or have none.
I have made a proposal to my heart
that if she will come back to me
I will declare war over and go home.

It will be a long night's parley.
In short she writes I cease delight
in fighting, end my part first, withdraw
into the country but I can't see how.

How may a man lay down his weapons
before others who envy him?
Merely for living I have enemies.
Useless to say I made them so.

And there it ends: in failure.
My heart won't come back now.
I draw the long wine from its leather.
I see the long night to its close.

Because of my kind nothing.
Issuant of me the long war
centuried and worse weaponed
than any wedge of longbow.

And finis. These cities
kindling to one furnace,
one tangle of astronomies,
one burn across the campagna.

Goodbye my heart. We fade
in different directions.
There will be less and less
we ever shared: the woods,

the distant terrafirma,
the cypress and the silver olive,
blue sky, white cattle,
measured out in fire,

all counted out in one
and time since Adam ashes
in the time it takes to read
and in the time it takes to tell.

It has already happened, the flash
winked out its message to the other stars,
the ink burned in the engraving, such record
as survived now in dispute.

Already pain has eaten through the page,
so many words gone into air
and we no longer here who dream
over and over the whistle at the finish.

Such is my bookwork: a contagion
of shadows, maps of warring neighbours,
border posts shifting in the candle flare,
white fire and the nothing I foresee:

the centuries of hate bloom there,
the paper in your hands is ash.
So goodbye to the voices in the alley.
So goodbye to the spiders in the wall.

So now I must step smartly
yet with long circumspection
through the last of the landscape
before the century collapses:

a tangle of cut limbs
burning on some bloody hill
where all ends in carnage
and pray God I've an advantage.

Pray I've taken the measure right
of the land's lie in my favour
and last in my skull as I die there
some mapwork of hedge and ditches.

I cheat none but a worse death
in some ratslicked dungeon
or dropped in the pesthole,
death's shilling in my armpit.

I shut the devils in their book,
I set the hellfire back into its star.
I plan to cross the littoral in good order,
swiftly and without my enemy knowing.

Between daybreak and candle sput,
a first blue light around the poplars,
between nightingale and cockcrow
dreaming I'm awake I dream my heart's dream.

And there we fly, in air sharp after rain
to evening water, two birds anywhere
across fields, the landscape pieced away
like the dropped jackets of soldiers.

And the wars over, the harvests
taken in order, history a meaculpa
not much happens, the images
of troops and weapons fading in the stone.

Thereafter little to report:
the business of good women,
tradesmen sleeping in their takings,
flags fading in cathedrals,

farmers and journeymen along the road
of the never ending landscape,
the continent at peace their country,
its government a distant rumour.

In the text known as *Where I failed,*
in the addendum *But we tried,*
directions to this place are fanciful,
the maps white terra incognita, or lost.

Etcetera etcetera. The ways of men
are combative, each locked in his defence,
his territory forever in himself
he carries in dispute, less space

than this the candle lit, a thing
no larger than his name he calls
his own true sovereign republic –
on the move, sharp, tough, and hungry.

My heart's caught in a thicket.
She has forgot to fly
and plays the lapwing's game.

I see her falling far away
in thorny quickset, bleeding
at the hands of strangers,

like me fading in the other lives.
Soon little will be known of us,
she with her dream of peace,

I hearing *blood more blood* in my ears,
still hunting for what bird
she's taken for her shape now.

There will be two seasons –
war then long winter.
There the tale ends.

I shall leave this place,
for choice without wailing
or fuss in the Italian manner.

Say of me if you can: a man
that kept his word at any cost,
trusted nothing less.

Goodbye England, *that nest of singing birds,*
tall ladders of the hearth smoke
climbing on the valley air.

Somewhere's an end to it,
the landscape leaning skyward,
the slow oncoming to the sea's edge.

And then the last page turned,
the candle finger thumbed into a smut,
the book shut and I tell no more.

Colden Valley

North I'm convinced of it: childhood's over,
in the narrow valley in the mist the frost
is silver in the veins and edge of leaves,
and last year's briar's coppered into stone.

Then more stone dragged to quarter fields
in which the miserable lives of beasts in winter
whiten into breath. The valley pulls –
poor pasture, poorer footage, water falling.

And all its children gone through millyards
into stone they chiselled *Billy, Emma, Jack,*
and gave their dates and shut the ground
in work and prayer. Or they are almost here,

their short days closing in an owl's hoot,
crows labouring over woods, along the road
a footstep always just about to fall
and all their voices just about to start.

Roads in the north between two seas

As ever, the straight track between trees
receding out of the eye of the painting
into brown distance, water, a haze
already forming on the vague hills, sky.

I am again in my own true country
that surely existed, a map in a drawer,
a postcard, a print in a seafront café,
a place it has always just stopped raining.

The macadam shines, two bands of emerald
are kerbside grass, trees in the wind
and the afternoon sunlight's arrival
down the prim brickwork of the avenue.

So much childhood: the sun's raw eye,
the northern sea grey and unlovable,
the swift constellations of birds
over the bayline, like silk's shine.

Like salt scattered across tables.
Like the Pleiades, some place we'll not go
past the flightpath of the terns,
the cold salt aching down the easterly.

Salt. Stiffens locks, the keys
jam in the doors, doors in their jambs,
the windows in the windworked shutters,
the widows stiffening in easy chairs.

Clear again is one moment, as to detail
precise in my imprecise memory, it begins
this long tale I am telling myself
as to why and who am I on this road.

I am six, I am getting in wood,
it is evening in winter, the ice
plates the horsetrough, in my hands
the sticks in the woodpile are frozen.

On the third step of the mounting block
there's a white milk can, waiting,
the air round and the winter stone
wear off the milk's heat: *the moment.*

We will die, all: my father, mother,
such kin and such friends as all love
and the world lends, and I
no exception fall out of knowing.

It was death looked at me then
in the white shadow in kindling,
a dark brief face in the ice,
the cold closing my fingers.

I broke sticks. The sun lay
over field frost. The farm clanked,
humming milk, moaning complaint,
long ago, its moment comes back now.

I am again under Orion, the moon again,
by the sea that returns everything lost
in the tide's rope tangled up, the birds
at the watery limits of the English.

I'm the sea gone sour, going radioactive,
betimes touchy as anti-matter, untouchable
in the north, I go down hissing
leukemia between the lovers' sheets, *the blood*

will wither in its artery, the sperm
shudder in the egg, the marrowbone,
the molecule unwind within the heart, the brain
stare into nothing and be dumb.

This is not a melody nor a tale told for children.
This is not a telegram to the poets in Minneapolis.
This is not an answer nor a question.
This is not a message. This is not a song.

Now we are travelling into Cumbria, the road
running out to water down the lost peninsula.
Now I am far away recalling winter and the fog
across another country, continent, biography.

When what I think to say is that we're done,
where everywhere is in the crosshairs,
everywhere is targeted, we are the printout,
we are the coded blips, we are the software.

'Filled with longing, capable of grief.'
Tough luck Susie Rainbow fare thee well.
She got the hero not the message, hostage
of a government that failed, my friends

this may be all too long a night along the road,
and I begin again. Again. I who left
everything behind I have forgotten nothing,
so it appears. With our desire we continue.

Grabbing any end of rope, we might be anywhere
or anyone under the blue star of evening
spreading out our maps, we might be
you and I my love and love each other.

A white sheet perhaps, the glance of shirts
across the winds of March, a glimpse
of washing in the gale in next door's yard,
the kitchen window staring into nothing –

soil, these fingers and these tongues
the crocus and the snowdrop put through frost,
a cat's dance through the cold we hoped
would grow to summer, last the flash

across the wind-whipped shrubbery,
the shed in fire, the glare that wastes us
with its glance, the crack of sheets
in wind, their sudden whiteness.

Commercial break: RSK Porsche

This is the dream: such distance
the oncoming wind is brother to,
long silk of the highway spun off
between the shoulders of the roadside.

All day the singing in tall weeds,
the grasshopper's confession, the birds
remembering their plainchant, reciting
little bread no cheese and the nine times table.

Some dawn the mist blows free, some
afternoon of dusty sunlight, the soundtrack
a far falling of a river over stones
Mozart's ear might have listened to.

West through willow country, villages
of woodsmoke sleeping in the valley,
or on the causeway through the lowlands
beneath the high white music of the larks.

Or anywhere. Across the upland,
sunset shimmering the treeline, gone
across the cobbles of the market,
the tall road only halfway to forever.

Communiqué from desk 19

One we've dissolved our office,
scrambled the files, regrouped,
our propaganda no longer exists

in which to deny *Two* the war's lost,
the phone book the new roll of honour,
it's not true we were beaten nor

Three we're dead meat now
in the deep stale air of the bunker,
our voices taping instructions:

What to do when the current runs out,
What to do with the blood, the world
taken down like a line of washing,

full stop. We're not here,
we're all moving on, some at work
on the new speech, the others

planning the deployments,
counting the syringes, the blankets,
the new ways to be nothing at all.

Lilith

Some far country she speaks from,
she was born there, can never go back
nor will where she lost.

Everything. The earth rippled
waves of the sea she tells.
Then soldiers, beat her and used her,
burned her house, broke everything.

Her man broken, her children, how
to get out then, *the airport broken,*
the ships. Suddenly again

the interrupted carpentry, the wheat,
the young trees and the apple
stopped in the blossom. Her complaint.

Het achterhuis

A glimpse: at the high window her face
a moment at a corner of the blind,
the frost forming its flower, in the garden
all the winter leaves so much leather,
so many tongues, scraps of old gossip.

For so little you can die: the price
on a second hand coat, a finger ring,
the brown shoes in the cupboard, the mirror
where your mother powders her face.
For these you will be taken.

Mice on the stairs, grey packets of dust.
The ice making its maps out of water.
On the square stones of the Prinsengracht
soldiers' boots tapping *links rechts links*.
In its season the chestnut's sudden blossom.

Letters from a lost uncle

Postcard of Chicago streets,
one blurred brown figure ringed in ink,
then written on the back *it's me now.*

Wherever he was then. He drifted west
along the railroad ties, went north
to work the dams, south to the rigs,

through Germany and the lowlands, spoke of Alaska
and the deserts of Arabia, he'd seen
more gold than all God's grains of sand.

But no one's heard in years, he may be dead
or changed, all memory of a life
he sometime lived blinked out like stars.

And all his laughter stopped, the voice
that rounded out in bitter beer
broke forth in *Crimond.* Where

does it go, that presence in the air,
brightness of a man that sang,
a breath that answered in his name.

Bogart in the dumb waiter

after Dashiell Hammett

This is genuine coin of the realm.
A dollar of this buys ten of talk.
The cheaper the crook the gaudier the patter.
I'll see you at the inquest maybe.

I'm a reasonable man. I don't mind
a reasonable amount of trouble.
All I've got to do is stand still
and they'll be swarming all over me.

More than idle curiosity prompts my question:
how'd you like to turn my chops over?
Yes. I'm tired of lying, tired of lies,
of not knowing what the truth is.

So listen carefully here's the plot:
the grieving widow walks on, grieves,
walks off again still grieving.
You want to hang around you'll be polite.

You get loose teeth talking like that.
You're taking the fall, precious.
If you're a good girl they'll give you life.
If they hang you I'll always remember you.

The shortest farewell's best: adieu.
Here's to plain speaking and clear understanding.
I distrust a close mouthed man. I'm a man
who likes talking to a man who likes to talk.

Three from the freak house

1.   THE TATTOOED WOMAN

On each arm a blue snake wrist to shoulder,
jaws apart, the long flicker of tongues
forked to each nipple, one lettered *mild,*
the other *bitter*. She's my snake lady,

the anaconda circling her waist, the cobra
rippling her belly, her neck a rattler,
each thigh a garter snake, her crotch a pit,
a snakey river many men have failed and fallen in.

On one rear cheek the anchor of the wandering sailor,
the other wears the lucky horseshoe of the landsman.
Above a skull a scroll spells out *forever love*
below a name scratched out she can't recall now.

2.   TIGER LIL

You won't remember me. I'm the one that tupped
in the wall in the brass bed in the next room
of your father's dream the night he sired you.
Not that your mother knew. No wonder you're stunted.

In my time I've fucked under flags of all nations
and all for the love of it, banging the bedsprings
from Cairo to Cardiff. I'm the same good whore
in every man's port, in a window in Amsterdam

where I sit behind glass in my credit card fur,
in my black suspenders and tigerskin chair.
And I show them my tongue. I show them my eyes
and my lilypad skin. And I purr.

3.   TOM PEEPER

My name's Tom Peeper, I live in Gropecunte Lane
among the other animals. Under this woolly cap
I'm entirely made up of the private parts of lovers
busy at each others' bodies in the ferns.

I'm a mixed bag of tits mouths cocks cunts
and little boy bums, I'm a sandwich of meat in meat
and I dream every night of the gold skins of women
naked among leaves with nipples like diamonds.

As for you. You never see me under the briars
in my charity shop cast off hush puppy shoes.
You're too busy. You come with a bird's fierce cry
in woods where the lovers are both one beast now.

Hatred of barbers

Imagine being anyone, a barber
for instance honing his razors,
shaking the tall white sheet
from its corners and sweeping.

All clippings and small talk,
a deft stroke from Saturday's game,
how weather is, how money,
the punchlines of six jokes.

His contempt, his power
to make any man ridiculous
in a glitter of scissors and mirrors,
one arm a brush then a hand:

You want anything Guv –
blades, rubbers, a change
(wink nudge) *is a rest.*
And then:
   When he gets there

When he kneels in the Sistine Chapel
with his missus for the blessing
on 20 years wedded bliss God's bailiff
the Pope says
    So who cuts your hair John?

The ballad of Eddie Linden at Earl's Court

When last I saw ye brother
you were falling on your face
as one copper then another
held you fast in his embrace.

We were halfway down the road,
we were halfway going home,
we were strangers in a crowd,
some of them in uniform.

Though none of us were virgins
and few of us were straight,
the constable and sergeant
had your number from the start.

And before the bust was through
and the punchup yet to come,
two gentlemen in blue
declared they'd have your bum.

Send in backup cried the jack
in his jacket radio.
*A hostile crowd is at my back
and they bid me let him go.*

And all in just a second,
in the space it takes to tell,
they came as they were beckoned
with the funny squad as well.

We were rapidly outnumbered,
oh the shame it is to think,
if we lingered we'd be lumbered
and we'd all be in the clink.

There was filth upon the street
and it took you for a ride.
You were just their kind of meat,
they were never on your side.

You were buggered from the off,
you were always on their books.
They never liked your stuff
nor much cared for your looks.

So they beat you black and blue
when the brown stuff hit the fan.
You were falling off the waggon
when they threw you in the van.

THE LONDON POEMS

After Mr Mayhew's visit

So now the Victorians are all in heaven,
Miss Routledge and the young conservatives
chatting with the vicar, visiting again
the home for incurables who never die.

The old damp soaks through the wallpaper,
there's servant trouble, the cook
fighting drunk at the sherry, and Edith
coughing and consumptive, fainting away.

Only this time it never ends: the master
continually remarking how the weather bites cold,
the brandy flask stands empty, and the poor
are pushing to the windows like the fog.

Encounter at St Martin's

I tell a wanderer's tale, the same
I began long ago, a boy in a barn,
I am always lost in it. The place
is always strange to me. In my pocket

the wrong money or none, the wrong paper,
maps of another town, the phrase book
for yesterday's language, just a ticket
to the next station, and my instructions.

In the lobby of the Banco Bilbao
a dark woman will slip me a key, a package,
the name of a hotel, a numbered account,
the first letters of an unknown alphabet.

The meridian at Greenwich

We find the river again, the ferry
south over the great water, on the shore
you read *Take Courage* and you're not joking.
In my fear the city, the blue misty planet

vanishes, a curtain ripped away
and nothing in back but fire, the river
and the busy roadway rolled aside
in our bad dreams from nights we don't sleep.

And no one to remember. No messages
passed late at night across borders, by hand,
by word of mouth, we who are lost together
telling tales the prisoner spins the jailer.

Movies after midnight

From Canning Town to Woolwich
the tall cranes rust. The pub's shut
and the lift's out in the towerblock,
everything you see is up for sale.

But there's a night movie: the well fed
soldiery with fancy weapons come
to stutter out the liberators'
brief philosophy: *up yours Commie.*

Even the prime numbers are giving up,
all the best words have moved to Surrey
and we have just a few at discount now
to make farewells that vanish with us.

In Silvertown, chasing the dragon

The police are called *Syncromesh*
wailing desolations on the flyover
playing the two tone music. Greetings
and goodnight from the kingdom.

Whose government is known as *sh*,
they own the miles of wire, the acids
that devour forests and white words out,
and they are listening in the telephone.

But we are all going away now
into some other dimension, we speak
a mirror speech there and count differently
and no one stands for the Queen any more.

Beyond hope and the Lea River

'She's five foot four and falling.
Either you come get her right now
or let her sleep it off in here
and we charge her in the morning.'

My friend Napoleon visits Farina's Café.
There is no message. He meets no one.
It is mysterious because there is no mystery
but Napoleon is now in the house of numbers.

We are entering the capital of a lesser empire
where the plans of our masters surface betimes –
pins on a map at the Ministry of Natural Calamities,
and the statistics like crisp new folding money.

Clipper service

In black and white the Isle of Dogs,
slow workless docklands going cheap,
the great outworks of power stations.
I'm living on two eggs and no bacon

here beside the river, smokey as ever,
among strangers. Ships there were son,
and lascars, then as now the afternoon
brought sulphur on the wind and no comfort.

Now the natives are proud and scattered
and lonely in the high rises, living
as they always lived: thieving or work
when there's work. There's none now.

Message on the machine

Your protagonist is not at home just now.
He's out, a one way window in his head
with everything coming in fast across the city
and always an alarm bell ringing in the buildings,

a jammed horn streets away, the town winds
lifting documents along the Broadway,
along Commercial Road a signboard
banging in the night reads *Smack*

Disposal Systems, he fears skinheads
in the drains and angels in the elevator
and the number 5 bus will never come now.
After the tone there will be a brief message.

Unfinished portrait

Today I'm Red Rover, late the Queen's
Own Leicester Square Irregulars, DSO
and several bars, and ageing in my trades.
Today I'm doing double glazing duty,

I'm on the weather watch, especially
for the Greek girls in Minnie Mouse shoes,
I'm with the CIA, I need a fix, say friend
how came we through the middle ages without whisky?

Henceforth I shall speak basic and fortran.
I'll say *excuse me sir I don't have a dog to walk.*
I'm primed, armed, fused, and now I'll tick
till I go off. Think of me as a deterrent.

Out West

Here is the moment holding its belly:
water swills from a main an iridescence
of spilled oil, the broken street
and scattered *this is raw human meat.*

Your man now is the frightened rabbit
fixed in the oncoming traffic, headlights
swirling the wet, the bleared music
of the squad cars and ambulance.

Caught in the shutter, run off
in the final editions: *you bastards you,*
and last in his last glimpse the rope
made of the hot blood spilling from his head.

Leaving the Angel

This far the trains are still running,
the night still awake. Then you're gone,
angry with me, late and lost in the city.
Love, our two furies will wreck us

blazing in the black space between.
I meet the man with seven omens there,
the one who sharpens knives and sings
in neon light *I put an edge to an edge.*

And I've encountered some river
of grieving in myself and drown in it,
living some days a half life on the stairs
defining *lonely* by not being there.

At the Barbican

Oh men she says, and means
their rigmarole, half truths
muttered half drunk on the home stretch.
There's always one man boasting in a bar

recalling how we slew the enemy
at Agincourt or in the far Malvinas
or spoke with Homer – still a boy
with others in the woods inventing stories –

changed, misremembered, *lies most of it,*
still bawling on the doorstep for his shilling,
bragging all the lives his conker has,
ridiculous, in short pants.

The talk at the big house

By nightfall when they hope no one's looking
the paramilitaries are out shifting fences
dressed in each others' uniforms. As intended
the signal from the government in exile

is opened by the wrong hands, so much lost
in the foreign tongue, so much of meaning
is a border always shifting in dispute.
No one gives an inch. No one affords it.

Then war, then peace, then normalisation.
The other side sends fraternal greetings.
The dissidents are hosed down hour on hour,
the guitar player's fingers smashed by rifle butts.

Dosser

I am says he *an exploited human being,*
half brother to these men at Charing Cross
sleeping in their cardboard apartments,
fighting in a line at dawn for work

if there's work scrubbing in the entrails
of the Ritz, and every man jack of them
upholds the free flow of market forces,
weary with his tale of dull misfortune.

I own two wrong shoes and a tartan blanket,
a spoon, a pencil, and my famous collection
miscellaneous plastic bags, my bequest
in lieu of taxes to the nation that bore me.

Slow dancer's epitaph

He was the black boy skating in the cars,
some city music on the headphones,
or at the video game, there being no other work.
He went to sea. He didn't want to die.

And on the radio that day a song of Souvla –
so long ago the bright lads sailed,
good men and ships blown in the water.
But he would go. I didn't father sons for this.

Soon he was hunting down the radar,
targeting the bloodbeat. By then
there was no other work for him,
no dance but shitting when the missile hit.

The house of the androgynes

We are invited. We're offered
tea or whisky, cushions, incense.
Their room is hung with damasks, shawls,
tall bowls of flowers, peacock feathers.

In love they have the music of each other,
their topics and a place they go in Portugal.
Later they promise indoor games: *the parcel,*
kiss the postman, chop your candle off.

All's softness and ambivalence, the air
breathy as recent sex. We say how like one
the other is as if two mirrors but which wife,
which husband, that we never figure out.

Of things past

I know they're never coming back now –
Malice Aforethought and Gay Abandon,
Sister Alabama of the Amateur Latin Americans
shedding her shoes for the compulsory dancing.

It's Sunday and World War 2 on four channels.
It's the fifth day of Christmas at a sick friend's.
I'm out giving my credentials an airing
and my provincial's contempt for the provinces –

little towns where there's no dancing.
I remember the sixties. In another life
we would be lovers living in the suburbs
making fickyfick and many bambinos.

Tube talk

She tells him her dream, she arrives
with a suitcase full of her poems
she's not written yet, her initials
in cursive tooled in the leather.

It's a wide angle lens. If you had
two chops you'd end up with two bones.
And the young barrister's speech *Sir*
I address myself last to the window.

When the open society closed I was drunk
your majesty. Now what I hear is random,
names back in use like *The Titanic,*
the heavy rhythm of the snatch squads.

Nobody's apartment

In the next place of the dream a voice
is beginning to whisper loud in the late
flicker of a TV nobody's watching:
razors available on request.

Nobody lives here. No one at all
remembers the next war. The buildings
whine in their own way their own adventures:
such a good building such a nice space.

And the pipes sing and the telephone rings
and the fridge tunes in its only song
about rented spaces and borrowed tuxedos,
but nobody's here that will fix me a drink.

Your friend the drifter

Too many years up and down the world
chasing some light that goes out.
She's always moved, the job turns out
to be some people talking in a train.

Some work up cures for new diseases,
some we never see decode our traffic.
Others are mapping the new dictatorships,
others the movies they will make of them.

But all night long I have been underwater
mining the harbours off Nicaragua,
I need a place to dress up in my uniform.
I have a deal for you. I'm your imaginary friend.

Talking with God

First the productivity agreement,
the vote of confidence, the loyalty oath,
then the standing ovation to mediocrity,
and still the powers that be are peevish.

What lies in the muddy bottom of the well:
curses rolled up in lead, fixed in a nail,
petty grudges and greedy prayers to be rich
or richer, the clenched fists of revenge.

And the words *How I rejoice in my enemies.*
You who gave out my secret, beware,
addressed to Minerva the owl
and for her eyes only, as if she were looking.

The window of vulnerability

Sure today it could come in a fast plane
named perhaps for the pilot's mother,
the city ends in a smear in the road
and that in a child's shoe. No one

will say aboard the Missouri *all these*
proceedings are now closed, by nightfall
hours beyond zero no one remarks
it was grey, it had no beauty at all.

Now what to do with these postal districts
drifting downwind? It would be
routine enough on the autopilot,
flying home till there's no home to fly to.·

A bad day at HQ

Today's not good. We are enduring
une abaissement du niveau mental. Next door
banging on the wall all night and now
everyone is looking, sliding in and out

the flat mercury of mirrors. We are perhaps
the last citizens of an imaginary country
hired to destabilise the client kingdoms,
write the royal speech at Christmas,

broadcast to the disabled nations
and vanish on a cruise to oblivion. Friend
we need a space, we need a stretch of air,
most urgently we need another walk in the woods.

Drinking at Dirty Dick's

Truth is I'm a prince among princes
with my own bit of a dukedom hereabouts
but my betters keep saying I'm a lizard,
a common reptile that understands nothing.

And I love the young princess, the way
she steps from the helicopter to bless
with her smile the disabled children
and cut the ribbon on the new hypermarket.

Otherwise my life is bad Danté, brown rice
or acupuncture, or waiting in the takeaway
for an order of dropped duck and noodles,
playing *Defend Cities* till it kills me.

The soldier's tale

What hit him was the pain, his hip
blown clean way they said, his bearers
argued in two foreign tongues which army
owned the blanket he lay bloody in.

Then he was going home. Someone
had put five Woodbines to his chest
and that was all his medal. The wife
was blitzed and took off with a fancy man.

He writes, *she was another beach*
where all my efforts were in vain.
The inscription on the back reads
the dead piled on the sea stones.

A case of medals

You find me sir, eleven of the a.m.
of a weekday drinking by myself good malt
with indifferent barley. I love a woman
but she's gone into another time zone.

I own a case of medals like a spicerack,
my days so many stars and wars there
with my dicky soldier's heart. I was a runner,
a disaster looking for a place to happen.

I've quit that. Somewhere the running
and the putting on of masks must end,
the tale turned dull and cloudy April
in the city, or will spring never come?

Absolutely no selling

I don't work she says on the top deck
in machine talk in a little girl voice,
a tape announcing the fault in itself
they say there's no cure for, over and over.

I could pack shelves in the supermarket.
I could calibrate the ages of the rain.
I could say again again *I can I know*
I know I can like the little red engine.

It comes to this: we will be happy,
we will laugh, we will be loved
some place we never come to, what we want
we will not have, and so goodnight prince.

The Botanic Garden Oath

Each of us, each with a tale to tell,
each one starring in the scenario called *me,*
sad for all the little of our lives
and all the short days of our loving.

But today I leave that out and take a train.
I've joined the Rupert Bear School of Poetry
and I'll not say anything controversial.
Here there's peace, the traffic tuned to a blur

and only the flightpath of the great planes
to disturb this fuchsia magellanica.
Especially I love the tropical conservatories,
their great ferns and the hot air full as sex.

Not talking on the Circle Line

for Judi

Let's take a slow dance on a fast train,
thee and I love, since all the news
is bad news, and now the radio
is yelling *gas gas,* and still the heart

delivers its message: *get on with it.*
Maybe I can work on the nuclear facility
or maybe I'll just wander off like Lao-tse
and disappear beyond the western frontier.

Or you and I could slip out anywhere,
take a walk around the park, a cup of coffee,
start the peace talks up again
and take the next train out of this place.

Person to person transatlantic

You're away, gone over the heavy sea
and *I miss you* is everything I say.
I say it *oh I love you* down the telephone,
the electronic chatter in the deep

sea cables at the bottom of the heart,
I bounce *I love you* off the satellite
and let the listeners in the circuits
make what they can of it, a code we know

for *I would take the world's end with you,*
we may have to, we know the state
conspires to kill us. Give us peace and to eat.
We hear it in the wires, the radio, the music

The John poems

I
And so: the cannons, the fountains, the fireworks,
the oratorio and the aerial display by the Red Arrows –
so educational, so good for the children – and last
the dawn chorus of the orchestra and the curtains:
here I am centre stage with a name like John
and hardly a damn thing to say for myself: merely
I am the man that can never spell straight,
the envoy of a country that won't negotiate.

II
I wake, I make my first tea in all the world,
surprised the downstairs and the kettle, three
green bottles on the windowsill are present
and correct, not vaporised in sleep,
the sirens weeping through the short night's
many possibilities: a line crossed, a wire
singing in the radar triggering the rockets.
I am awake, the blackbird's song against the sky.

II
I have been walking my domains, where everything
and nothing much has changed. I have been here before.
I have a photograph of who I was then, standing
ill at ease in a borrowed suit of clothes
in the room of bleached light, one workman's hand
across the chairback, the other halfway to his waistcoat,
the silver Albert and medallion on whose clasp
there is no timepiece, but only I know that.

IV
Most of us with little, a christening spoon
or on the wall a souvenir of some daft war
our grandfathers had died in, before the sperm
homing on the egg on a 48 hour pass from Boulogne
burst all their passion through us to our children,
here in the rainy kingdom, in the long peace
fought for in another country. For my inheritance
I had a pair of copper cufflinks, now my son's.

V
I have examined the leader's brain with my nightprobe
finding not much but fear of God and strong language,
random events I have no vision or power to read.
We are got ready for war again it seems, the hiss
of air released again from the dead, and the band
going down with the ship playing *Abide with me*.
I'm jumpy when the allies practise mass graves,
or when a truck goes by that says *the real thing*.

VI
Listen. Everything is still as a Dutch painting,
forever Sunday. I'm a man clearing space round himself,
one hand signalling the gods, the other a gardener
of balm and sweet savoury, living my secret biography,
my name and a self addressed stamped envelope
by return of post: John with his book of anyone,
his bell and light, his exit left, his tall tale
as to our masters' thinking and where grow weeds.

VII
This moment now someone is mining the waterway,
closing a frontier, someone is arming the missile,
someone makes love, makes a profit, an objective analysis,
someone is torturing someone with telephone wire,
someone is listening, this is routine someone says.
The women join hands at the chainlink fencing,
the convoys the colour of gangrene sneak out at night,
the microwaves weeping out messages we can't read.

VIII
The president is in his rose garden. I in mine.
All afternoon discussing Armageddon with the evangelist,
he's thinking dammit time to open the good book
and strike first, the work of a moment meanwhile
to admire the fuchsia coxinia, the lawn, the tea rose
opening itself, the white blaze of the magnolia.
Here in the same moment it's dusk, my love and I
plant marigolds, alyssum and night scented stock.

IX

We talk of another rose garden, by the long shore
you call home. Your mother, call her the rose lady,
grows blue flowers there, the shade her eyes
and the seas possess. *I have the truth* you say
but where the hell's my purse? Tonight we drink,
we may weep over the floor if we want to. Always
the low itch in the skull to give up, to forget,
go crazy and keep running till the heart bursts.

X

Always on the shore of great events, almost a witness,
or are we merely a reserve set well apart
in some cupboard in the suburbs working out
our dangerous purposes, here at the finish.
Caught in the playback I'm the man with *Time Out*
walking the square the moment the other world's
ambassador opens up with a machine gun: that man.
I'm the missing witness. And they never ask.

XI

The nights end in cat fights and backyard wars,
bad dreams and between a little night music perhaps,
a little work experience. East of the city
the missions are still preaching boxing for boys
and the evils of drink. West at Kew the mandrakes
in their glass mausoleums form my last exhibit,
last offspring of the city's hanged men, last blip
across the cardiogram across the city's narrative.

XII

That's it then officer I'm John with my invisible.
I keep changing my name to fox the government.
I'm John with my music plain speech down at heel
making a muzak of everything, the ice cream bell
and the roar of the crowd risen up, and the sea
on the beach stones that are all wearing white
for the evening. Officer, I'm one among others,
every day we are more and we're all called John.

IGNORE PREVIOUS TELEGRAMMED EMOTIONAL OUT-
BURST. ● THAT OF ITSELF PROVES NOTHING LIKE
LEUKEMIA. ● YEARS OF COPIOUS ENQUIRY WILL
VINDICATE MY WORDS. ● I'M THE MINISTER FOR ST
ELMO'S FIRE AND I REPEAT ● IGNORE PREVIOUS UN-
SUPPORTED BIAS. THE GOVERNMENT SAYS ● IT'S OK
THE RAIN ISN'T EATING THE FOREST. WE THINK ●
SOME TOPSOIL MAY REMAIN AND SOME OF US SUR-
VIVE ● OCCASIONAL NUCLEAR HOLOCAUST. THESE
MATTERS SUB JUDICE ● NATIONAL SECURITY SUB-
JECT OF COURSE TO A D NOTICE ● AND THE USUAL
THIRTY YEAR RULE, THE FILES DEEP IN THE MOUNT-
AINS, ● THE LONG TAPES WHISPERING IN THE NIGHT-
WEBS, ALL SAFE ● IN THE HANDS OF OUR ALLIES THE
WHITE MALE ANGLO SAXON ● PROTESTANTS OF
NORTH AMERICA, SOME ALREADY BORN AGAIN. ● END
OF ANNOUNCEMENT.

IGNORE PREVIOUS TELEGRAM

The Olympic Year

She was a dancer and I loved her once,
perhaps again. I was loyal as the London plane tree.
I simply thought of her to save a phone call.

He was another runner in the relay sprint,
the wind behind him twice the legal limit,
a new breed with an edge running from the front.

How many broken records and a medal, secret letters
from the unknown Tasmanian in the shot-put?
Let's say a normal sort of life, *o solo mio*
on the ice cream vans when all the war breaks out.

Agie's advice

You don't have to insist on being yourself.

Never make decisions on the road.

Never put your papers on the table.

And never count your money in the wind.

The actor

I'll close the window he said over the telephone.
Someone may hear us. Ignore my previous telegram.
I've played Lear in Hamlet and the fool in the Royal George,
I've played Departure, Rumour, Exit, Jack the Lad
and the buffet car from Paddington to Penzance,
the lodgings always filthy and the trains late,
stuffy and over full from Clacton to far Wigan's shore,
the whisky in the taproom always watered down.
I never had an encore, never saw a proper script.
From the tyranny of everyone sweet Mother defend us.

Eva's story

The other woman with the other man.
The kind of man that bites the bullet that feeds him.
The kind of woman keeps her orgasms under her breath.
Him saying *I can be a behaviourist if I want to.*
Hers the kind of cake he can't eat all of anyway.
Him with a wife and a wedding ring and a pussycat.
She in a portrait of wind in a white straw hat.
He with nowhere to go, no one to go there with.
She with no one to show it to, nothing to sing.
He was an actor she said, asked to stay a while.
Just a couple of boxes, a trunk. Six years ago.

Autumn with full summer

He's from the department of offers she can't refuse.
The plot is the same as ever: need of privacy,
love of solitude, fear of loneliness. The locale
contemporary London or Truth or Consequence New Mexico.

She knows he's gone beyond his shelf life.
Way past his due-by date. Mother knows it.

Old Westerns

So tell me what use is a stagecoach to an Indian?
My money's on the pony express getting to Laredo.
Does it have a zipper, does it have enough pockets?
Can you take it home and make a lamp out of it?

He's stuck with the myth of wandering herdsmen,
moving by stars between pastures and women.
Summer in another country. In the mountains.
I guess it killed him. How would he know?

How to get a job

Be prepared to work hard the first million years or so
banging about by the buildings asking *what's this for?*
Expect little pay and overcrowded conditions.

You should have been born clever.
You should have been born rich.
You should have been born in Saffron Walden.
You should have worked in school and considered
the example of the future Sir Robert Maxwell.

If you get an interview don't sniff any glue.
You will be offered less than the whole ten pence.
And wear a tie.

Two parts haiku

This was my first love:
the numerous wind through grass.

The Russians

Ignore all previous. We are totally surrounded
by dark shaggy bears, mad drunk on honey and vodka.

The program

Ignore previous couplet. Recode. Reprogram.
Reenter at line 69. Enter: *I'll be myself.*
I get in trouble being anyone else.

At the rostrum

If you speak up what to say but everything?
You will have a medal stitched to your chest.
You will be called a hero of the silent republic.
You'll be its spokesman brought home in a glass coffin,
given a state funeral and a very fancy motorcade.

Better sit close to the wall o mi amigo,
dealing the cards tight to the chest as they say,
hanging on to the hat and the pistols well oiled,
a silver .45 bullet clenched between the teeth,
what passes for a smile the bitten leather of my lips.

The 1984 Tour of Britain

Miners hunted down the corn by the mounted division.
Sad poverty's lament around the garden festival.
There's work in nuclear construction and security.
And yet much bitterness in the land of the butter mountain.
Sad junketing around the wine lakes. And here
the missiles we can't see move in their circles
on a page deleted in the interest of national security
while we were standing round in groups of one or less.
But we shall build Jerusalem. Well worth a visit.

Visiting Americans

So the other side dropped out of the guessing games.
Our runners compete best in non anabolic steroid events.
Just the athletic urine samples are a security headache.

I'm aware none of this means anything or just more guns.
I guess I'm a cynic. What use is this program?
That of itself proves nothing like smoking and cancer.
I was born in California but left no forwarding address.

If she marries him he'll be a non resident alien spouse.
She just loves London, spent the whole two weeks in Harrods.
Surely money's not the problem. Doesn't everyone?

Think I'll make me some money John, a whole piece of it.
Go live in New Mexico in maybe Truth or Consequences,
eat peyote and breed me some ponies.
Did you ever fuck a horse, John?

The previous telegram

She's gone at last leaving her honey musk
in the white room of their athletics, and no
forward address, no final note, no valediction.

I find her white straw hat with no ribbon,
some stray hair of her head, one blue shoe.
On my breath the mint of adultery, on my mind
the total recall of her skills on me. I send
c/o the wind two red roses and a telegram:

If you vanish I'll appear. If you go away
I'll materialise one sunrise on your doorstep,
I'll find you in your sleep. Across a square
my face will be familiar in some city, country
in whichever life, a voice a mouth you will recall.
There will be partings but no end to this.

Message from the Basque country

Give yourself the benefit of the doubt: nuclear power
is killing you. We have no crock to brew it in,
no bucket to contain the power of the sun.
What we get's more wire and chainlink fence,
another 32 varieties of police, more secrets,
more prisons and more central government –

and less and less the wild country to go to,
less and less the seas and rivers.
And there is nowhere for the waste.

Daft as a brush, Mother says.

The black report

Ignore previous telegrammed emotional outburst.
That of itself proves nothing like leukemia.
Years of copious enquiry will vindicate my words.
I'm the Minister for St Elmo's Fire and I repeat
ignore previous unsupported bias. The government says
it's OK the rain isn't eating the forest. We think
some topsoil may remain and some of us survive
occasional nuclear holocaust. These matters sub judice
national security subject of course to a D notice
and the usual thirty year rule, the files deep in the mountains,
the long tapes whispering in the nightwebs, all safe
in the hands of our allies the white male Anglo Saxon
protestants of North America, some already born again.
End of announcement. Perhaps later in the day
there will be a recital of *o solo mio* on the bicycle bell,
to be followed by the Didcot Sinfonietta of massed sirens
playing *Bye-bye blackbird* for barbed wire and geiger counter.
There will be scattered outbursts of caesium and strontium,
showers of alpha gamma beta followed by a very bad smell,
scattered backgrounds where loving anyone may be difficult.
It's OK the language isn't really a disease like Windscale.
In any case the place is called Cellophane or Sellafield.
They make only spare parts there and routine replacements
for several of the bad dreams you've been having.

Bonnie over the ocean

En route from elsewhere with some rare diseases.
She's a very sick puppy and ought to be in quarantine
but nothing stops the peace train or the pony express.

Oh they know what it is she says.
Except they never heard of it and gave the Latin name.
There is no cure, no treatment and no charge.

On exotica you get no better price per pound, Bonnie.
I say you're not guilty of anything but love.
You don't have to take the medicine.

Conditions in the west

It is the first condemned building in North America,
a bar on Third Avenue, lunch. Ignore stage direction.
If you got an imagination it's the ham and barley soup
you want we don't have. This guy came in I said Mother
he's either a very good customer or an asshole.
So maybe he did coach the San Diego Graverobbers,
Quasimodo for quarterback, Quetzalcoatl running back.
Anyway I was right. He is an asshole. *To the bank
to the bank to the bank* the tall man with the stetson
is singing his winnings on the pony expressway.
You think those Indians wanted that stagecoach?
Check the zipper on this whisky, check the pockets,
check can you take the bottle home, make love to it,
will it sing, will it write a sonnet, will it fly,
will it stack the storm windows in the basement,
cut the lawn, clear the bitter snow in winter,
will it keep you warm in age and will it last?
There's a thing to own a sweater outlasts the girl
that knitted it oh years ago and do you know her name?
Every Tuesday I get even. Today is Tuesday.
For a living I design meats. This ham & barley soup
Mother makes. She knits it underwater, naked,
singing *Oh Susanna* weeping for the world we inhabit.
The Russians are right: stay drunk. I've come to think
the tall guy lives a sheltered life under the hat
but then I never saw the movie. Next thing I know
his wife's calling on the phone from New Hope Pennsylvania
shitface come cut my grass or I'll disable you.
There's no reply but I keep knocking on the third drink.
What can you say to *Mein Vater war in dem SS?*
So what it's the Olympics with only half a medal?
When does the stagecoach event happen? With Mother
you could have your cake and eat it but you can't.
And then this crazy killer with a car, the creep
shoots out McDonald's and wanders off the porch
with a cool can of beer in his fist. And this:
this is Mother's soup the 23rd today and you know what
it's like the 23rd psalm it just ain't hot enough,
it ain't like Mother.

She checks her waitress pad,
takes down the order, stares beyond the window
past the bar strip's neon signature of city skyline,
Manhattan deep in elevator shafts, the haze
of traffic darkened air, the splutter in the airwaves,
peripheries of speech turned advertising copy,
the wordy trains a babylon of territories and codes
that make the fast train anyplace, the women
on the sidewalk minding their own sweet business –
and speaking of the valley of the shadow Mother says
and gets the soup. West of her is heartbreak country.
Fifty states of paranoia. *And that* the barman says
is a sign of good health round here. I'd say the map's
unreadable but I'm a stranger in these parts, a man
under his hat moving his shoulders in embarrassment
and looking tough among the towers of speech. I'd say
the trains and scribble in the subway. I'd say
between the whisky sours and ham and barley soup
the language is on fire, shot, taken out, erased
with extreme prejudice, irradiated, burned away.
I'd say the stagecoach. I'd say the previous telegram.
I'd say the elevators or the wailing chasm of the city.
I'd say the sirens. I'd say I'm out of signs
and running from the front when all communication cuts.

Nielsen's visit

Meanwhile in London Nielsen comes to call.
On the river bank a boot a bottle a wine bucket.
Old brown sails in the seawind by the Prospect of Whitby.

In another life Nielsen we were mates thumped drunk here,
and woke together in the Queen's Navee.

You want to know what Ezra Pound said to me?
He said *Thankyou* and walked off in the railway dark
of another black Italian night in his cape and cane.

Pound. Proud. From Wabash College. Weary.

Living with the boss

Don't tell me objects don't have feelings.
They resent our intelligence and fall down.
Telephones and police are never when you need them.

How did it get way past midnight without my noticing?
It's enough having to remember all day who I am,
how important, my number, my callsign, my cues,
where I keep the suicide pills and the silver bullet.

Am I or am I not the President of the United Shirts?
Did I accept this part? I have to call my agent.
I have to remember all this only to forget it
night after night with Nancy, and no let-up.

The space salesman

He's wearing a grey suit and not at all like Richard,
and he wants to talk to you dear. In confidence.
He says he's from the New Church of the Holy Loft Insulations
conducting a survey for the University of Double Glazing,
and this joke's wearing thin. He dines out
on his famous namesake and he's famous for it. I hear
her say oh years from now I was depressed my time there.
I guess I loved him. But there was never anyone at home.

Snobby Roberts' message

You're wrong she says. You'll do it my way.
I'm the head girl and all this democratic stuff
is for the firing squad and a short sharp shock
at the back of the gym with a rubber truncheon.

No cure. No treatment. No natural justice.
We have a business to run here. Sell everything.
Give the miners a stiff course in how to sink.
The prefects will know what to do with their hockeysticks.

I think she's never been lived in, Mother says.

Remembering the Fifties

So there I was with an open heart and a closed mind,
in love with the dancer. So where are you now,
the brown Armenian from the house of women?

I barely knew what language to tremble in.
I was in love suddenly with Italy, with Venice,
her many masks and silks and lace, her musks
and all her yellow birds singing in the water city.

A *city against nature* Chateaubriand called her.
I too danced and sang, a silver weathercock
strutting the Riva where I spoke with Benveniste's doppel
and went about sniffing the insides of tombs.

A normal sort of day, a typical existence
eating mayonnaise and pickles, the sweet red wine
uncocked an hour before dinner, and a fine view
across water to Our Lady of the Perpetual Erection.

I heard women calling from windows *Droppa your breeches*,
the sign across the waterway translating *Two Men Pissed here*,
and on the gramophone the voice of Signor Primatur Seniliti
when war broke out and ended all at once.

Graffiti in the hall of athletes

'Rajid Patel is a puff.' That gets everyone.

Good boys, all educated. All good clean girls
in clean white sheets. But no reward for being good
and I was never any good at being bad.

I fuck and sign her, cross the *t* and dot the *i*,
and dream the fat rain singing in the applemint.

Long distances

Her man's away beyond the mountains,
always moving with the herd. But he visits,
sends money, word of himself in other travellers.
Some of whom love her also. And she them.

The relay runner

Delete *rain*. Delete *applemint*. Delete *f*ck*.
I have to get in touch with my controller.
I have to plug myself back into the electricity.
I have to check in with my Earth Station.

He is running, he is running, the faces of the crowd
like water scattered in the sun, all eloquence
a blur across the wind in the distant city of the angels,
the fiefdoms of the Barreras and the White Fence Gang.

He's pumped with cortisone and anti-inflammatory.
This boy needs rest and more rest sing the airwaves.
He hands the baton on. Dark lady of the sonnet,
by now you will have guessed: all we ever do is gesture.

Disco dancing in Streatham

He's shot naught a bob or three that one.
War man than one in his wifetime can kink of.
Here comes the music.

Ah sweet land of green money. Such a life
put together of posters and signs, gestures,
images in the TV flicker of another continent,
another decade, stars of stage and screen,
characters in movies, all good consumers,
loyal citizens in borrowed dialogue
and borrowed clothes bearing urgent news
as to what's on and who's wearing it
in languages that don't compute.

Reasons why they met, reasons why they parted,
never reasons why they were together.

To exorcise a blackbird

You say OK blackbird that's far enough.
You say OK I'll give you the plot but the treaty's off.
You say you missed the point lady. The butler did it,
or the barman with the ham and barley soup.
You missed the joke about the stagecoach.
You remember the retired schoolmistress?
You remember the deserted cottage on the estate?
You remember the laird back wounded and blind from the war?
He fathered her a child and called her *princess*
once in his terrible dark, perhaps again. That child
became the priest in the black cummerbund and dog collar,
clicking his lilywhite fingers whistling sanfairyann
at the end of the performance but you never got it.
I've had it with your Olympics. You wore the medal out.
Ignore previous marriage. Ignore telegram.
There will be no midnight release from the tower
where the virgin sleeps unkissed. These days
she's working a funfair sideshow on a block of ice
always melting. Stay off my territory blackbird.

Gone for gold

Faithless. Alone and fatherless, a long starry highway.
Here's John again with his chat in and out of uniform
serving with the blood and guts brigade, cocky,
fly and unreliable. Don't depend on him, Sunshine.

He'll do a runner, change his name, reappear
in Stratford Langthorne living with another woman
as McGinty, Bartollini, Juan Day Sam the noodlevendor
selling 32 kinds of ice cream and home improvements.

Suburb city

Men tidying Sundays in their backyard sheds,
the nails and screws assorted in their boxes,
the hooks and fishing flies laid up for winter,
all the windfalls picked, the soil turnéd over.

The things women put up with from men and stay sane,
enthusiastic even. She imagines his private parts
and walks into the nettles. She keeps going back
to the source of the inflammation.

Maybe she can get a discount on her next life.
He frames her photograph and all his thought of her
twisted into loops of picture wire with pliers,
hung in any of the last rooms he will rent.

Departure's speech

Words like rain in the applemint. In my trade
I'm a journeyman living the life of waste nothing,
odds picked in skips, scraps my dead father kept,
all the words I can steal so look out for yourself,
my sisters, my brothers. I'm Thief, Joker, Twister,
Departure the weathergrained theatrical beached
at the Colony more often than not weeping in whisky
muttering *stagecoach, vulva, rain in the applemint,*
anarchist-in-waiting to the republic of survival.
For intance I might say *dry white Chablis pray*
and the barmaid reply *we've only dry roasted.*
They were led out in groups of five by the interpreter
across St James' Square. An ordinary sort of weather,
the usual sort of planet. Sir Officer Your Honour
I worked hard and drank only in *The Onlie Running Footman,*
he that cries the road clear before Their Lordships,
and takes the brickbats, sods, clods, sundry turds.
Now it seems I'm in trouble and nothing makes sense.
I've a severe condition of the gyratory system,
my inner ring road's clogged, I have flyover,
underpass, roundabout and Blackwall Tunnel.
I've been hammered in Hammersmith and Battersea,
I'm Tooting and Barking and Ealing and Southend,
I've Epping and Ongar head to foot, White City
and Parsons Green and probably terminal Shoeburyness.
I'm a sick puppy going home on the 12.15 to sleep.
For thirty pence you get at least one sort of cheese.
I'm a stone too light for its weight and full of holes.
I'm on the blink and fading fast. In the French
I thought I saw Chicago but I think he's dead now.
I closed the window on the telephone just in case.
I am become the destroyer of worlds Vishnu himself said.
For the loss of one day one thousand years regret.
By the omission of a letter, the variation of a constant.
In a sense we're all dead already Milton Keynes says.
And in another we begin every one by crawling.
Thank Christ I've recovered my deadly composure,
found my thread again, forgotten my euphoria.
I'm just a normal sort of crackpot. Do ignore me.

Throw me out if I snore, if I bore or offend
or raise two fingers to the photograph of T.S. Eliot.
I've been all over England, to Scotland and Penzance,
I died in the Winter Gardens when I saw the ladies dance
(– and pray to think they will dance for me again).
I made a mistake the first time around and settled
for a pair of tits. Her body. Designed I thought
to make men mad, but she's actually her own business
taking the late air along the Broadway. *Pig.*
What use is a stagecoat to an Indian in any case?
Who played the Bartender, and who took Mother's part?
So now you're all here ignore all previous telegrams.
Delete *applemint*. Delete *cruise missile*,
delete *Brook Street Girl*, delete *one blue shoe*,
delete *and oh the runny honey of her labia.*
And cut the sexy stuff. Pretty soon now
I shall deliver my treatise *Language as the Management
of Sexuality,* bored as ever with my Ph.D notes.
Truth is I'm a Wally with a Walkman listening to tapes
of his own voice in the subway, metro, underground,
tube. Once upon a time this was a live performance.
Once I was a puppy, a young poetrie apprentice
in the school of Whingeing Willy's blighted adolescence.
Now I get snotty letters from the likes of Anthony Thwaite,
my line is overextended. Is there no end to this?
Will no one switch me off, unplug me at the wall,
disconnect the supply or seal me in a vacuum flask?
Will no one tow me out to sea and sink me at night,
shoot me into space or the pony out from under?
I'm probably the ideal consumer. A million dollars
and a piano don't speak to each other at all
Quincy Jones says. I'm caught in the rain's graph.
I'm riddled with statistics, toxic, overtaxed,
overloaded, I've barely enough bytes for the program.
I'm contaminated and there's no discount, no treatment,
no Latin for it and no charge. Will the planet
recover from our wounds? Will the pony rider
make it to Las Cruces? Will Ronnie Armageddon
swat the planet flat and go to heaven in a sheet
and all the believers meet in the rapture?
Send now for catalogue. It's in the standard.
See it in the mirror in the news in the times

that's fit to print. Tune this channel next week
to the same exacting performance. In the privacy
and comfort of your own home blow your own head off.
Telegram your representative urgent soonest express.
If not the world save Venice, mother of poets.
For sure there's trouble in my mill. Surely
the government can do something. I'm lost
in all this complex electronic weaponry to defend me.
What if anything at all goes off, the wrong goose
in the wrong radar in whatever management of error?
May I enquire the name of this place, strange,
dangerous, the centre we suppose of what is known
of spacetime, on every side the anxious citizens
each with his and her different map of the district.
Till now I was content, my voice singing me to sleep.
We need peace Mr President, and quiet conversations.
And for vegetables a patch of good land Mr Chairman,
if the soil be workable, the ground cover sufficient,
the radiation in retreat, the sniper fire fading,
the depredations of the mercenary bands less and less
till year by year we reinvent the wheat, the spinning jenny,
the working of the differential gear and the sonnet.
I fear the program ends abruptly, one day the stereo
playing o solo mio in the city where the other woman
with the other man is waiting for the right bus
at the wrong stop when farewell all the rain:
the rider never makes it with the message, the words
roll off the page's edge like lemmings to the sea,
the marathon goes on forever with these jogging men
somehow puffing through the long nuclear winter.
How shall I find you in your sleep to whisper
there would otherwise be partings but no end?
Your eyes are soon enough, love. Ask what song
Mother sang us all to sleep with. Speak again
as Lear spoke and the dead in Homer, called again
beyond the ditch's lip to be an upright bag of blood.

THE ADVERTS

Ken Smith is a poet of formidable range and strength who has absorbed the life and landscape of America as well as that of Europe and of his own Yorkshire background. He cultivates a voice which is personal, yet much more than personal: the result of having opened up hidden layers of common fear, suffering and desire.
● **CHICAGO SUN-TIMES/Ralph J Mills**

His images read as if they were wrenched from the innards of his own experience and his verse manages to communicate on a basic, visceral level.
● **THE SCOTSMAN/Alan Bold**

THE POET RECLINING is Ken Smith's Selected Poems. It includes his major long poem <u>Fox Running</u>.

● HEAVY BREATHER

Ken Smith is so unswervingly serious a poet, such a heavy breather down the line to intensity.
● **THE OBSERVER/Peter Porter**

Recently, Smith has written increasingly important verse in which, in a less critical but more trenchant manner, he threatens even Larkin as a leading social poet. His sequence **Fox Running** is as important as Hughes's **Crow** poems as an innovative group.
● **TRIBUNE/Martin Booth**

● **Ken Smith**: 'common fear, suffering and desire'

THE POET RECLINING

● R A D I C A L   P R O S E

IF YOU LIKE HIS POEMS, you'll love his prose: extraordinary fictions, fables, ill-tempered jokes and (wait for it!) existential romances. Smith writes in the radical European/American (and most unEnglish) tradition of Borges, Brautigan, Burroughs and Buster Keaton.

● Smith's Chinese Whispers are: **Atmospheric Railway** ● **The History of Stones** ● **Island Called Henry the Navigator** ● **Anus Mundi** ● **The Wild Rose** ● **Not Quite Buster Keaton** ● **Ektachrome** ● **One of Our Objects Is Missing** ● and **Casual Labour of Sidmouth, Budleigh Salterton, Exmouth, Exeter and Districts Roundabout Unite to Form the Yetterton and Collaton Raleigh First Pragmatic Idealist Suicide Potato Picking Brigades Dedicated to the Overthrow of Everything Nasty** ●

● As in the game of Chinese Whispers, messages are passed, repeated, misheard, misremembered, deliberately tampered with, fiddled with in the interests of politics, commerce and the pursuit of power. Even the language is suspect. So are our perceptions.

● This stunning book is illustrated with mysterious pictures of sub-reality.

A BOOK OF CHINESE WHISPERS

KEN SMITH

BURNED BOOKS

should be etched on every poet's heart, or failing that, the study wall: 'don't lie to those people within you, they'll find out'.

● PN REVIEW/Ian McMillan

● SHATTERING LINES

This volume pretends to be the surviving fragments of a library assembled by President Perdu, an elitist dictator whose fall from power was attended by the mysterious firing of his collection. The very structure of the book is teasing, for our image of the despot relies on snippets and clues to his character from the salvaged remains of his taste, and some of his own compositions.

● THE LITERARY REVIEW/David Profumo

Witty pieces combine with gleaming fragmented poems like 'From Belmont, A Ghetto Song', with its shattering lines: 'On the wall a child's scrawl/ I hate me', and 'They never complain/ to whom nothing is promised', and, from 'Nicholson's advice', lines which

Lives ago, years past generations
perhaps nowhere I dreamed it:
the foggy ploughland of wind
and hoofprints, my father
off in the mist topping beets.

Where I was eight, I knew nothing,
the world a cold winter light
on half a dozen fields, then
all the winking blether of stars.

Before like a fool I began
explaining the key in it lost locked box
adding words to the words to the sum
that never works out.
                        Where I was
distracted again by the lapwing,
the damp morning air of my father's
gregarious plainchant cursing
all that his masters deserved
and had paid for.
                     Sure I was
then for the world's mere being
in the white rime on weeds
among the wet hawthorn berries
at the field's edge darkened by frost,
and none of these damned words to say it.

I began trailing out there in voices,
friends, women, my children,
my father's tetherless anger, some
like him who are dead who are
part of the rain now.

● BEING THE THIRD
   SONG OF URIAS
From THE POET RECLINING

BURNED BOOKS

THE POETRY IS NOT ENGLISH. It has escaped from the bounds of insularity and is not only universal in content but also wide in appeal . . .

His poetry is primal and basic . . . **Fox Running** uses a period of breakdown to construct a series of poems about a poet lost in the metropolis of slums and poverty, seeking himself and a way out of his inner and outer states of destitution. This may sound selfish and narrow, but Smith is never that. **He writes to people rather than for them** and it is upon this that he must base a good deal of his success. It might also account for his having been outside in the poetic wilderness for many years, unheeded by editors and many of his peers alike. **He is frankly too good** and must pose a threat to others.

● From **BRITISH POETRY 1964-1984: DRIVING THROUGH THE BARRICADES** by **Martin Booth** (Routledge, 1985)

● **Ken Smith**: 'He is frankly too good'

● **Ken Smith** was born in 1938 in East Rudston, Yorkshire, the son of an itinerant farm labourer. He has worked in Britain and America as a teacher, freelance writer, barman, magazine editor, potato picker and BBC reader, and has held writing fellowships at Leeds University, Kingston Polytechnic, and Clark University and Holy Cross, Worcester, Massachusetts. While living in America he served a term as poet in the Toledo House of Correction. He is now writer-in-residence at Wormwood Scrubs prison. His first book **The Pity** was published by Jonathan Cape in 1967, and his second **Work, distances/poems** by Swallow Press, Chicago, in 1972. Poems from these two collections and from numerous other books and pamphlets published between 1964 and 1980 (including **Fox Running**) were brought together in his Bloodaxe Selected **The Poet Reclining** (1982). Also available from Bloodaxe are his **Abel Baker Charlie Delta Epic Sonnets** (1982) and **Burned Books** (1981). His prose pieces are collected in **A Book of Chinese Whispers** (1986).

KEN SMITH